DRUGS AND THE PRESSURE TO BE PERFECT

Striving to look your best is healthy, but believing you must look "perfect" can cause you to put unreasonable pressure on yourself.

THE DRUG ABUSE PREVENTION LIBRARY

DRUGS AND THE PRESSURE TO BE PERFECT

Michael B. Langer

THE ROSEN PUBLISHING GROUP, INC.
NEW YORK

Published in 1998 by The Rosen Publishing Group, Inc.
29 East 21st Street, New York, NY 10010

First Edition

Library of Congress Cataloging-in-Publication Data

Langer, Michael (Michael B.)
  Drugs and the pressure to be perfect /
Michael Langer.
    p.   cm. — (The drug abuse prevention library)
  Includes bibliographical references and index.
  Summary: Discusses perfectionism and its causes, the possibility of its leading to drug abuse, and ways to cope with both problems.
  ISBN 0-8239-2552-8
  1. Teenagers—Substance use—Psychological aspects—Juvenile literature.   2. Substance abuse—Psychological aspects—Juvenile literature.
3. Perfectionism (Personality trait)—Juvenile literature.   [1. Drug abuse.   2. Perfectionism (Personality trait)]   I.   Title.   II. Series
  HV4999.Y68L35   1997
  362.29'11'0835—dc21   97-17522
                                                          CIP
                                                          AC

Manufactured in the United States of America

Contents

Introduction

*M*arco wanted his first date with Sabrina to be perfect. He had worked up the confidence to ask her out after hesitating for three months. Once she accepted, he couldn't stop worrying about the date. He bought a new shirt and shoes for the occasion, hoping that she'd like them. He wanted to look just right for his date with Sabrina.

The night of the party, Marco spent hours getting ready. He looked in the mirror. His hair was too short on top. Why had he had it cut like that? He should have left it longer. Marco put on a pair of gray pleated pants. He noticed that the crease didn't lie right in front. He spent twenty minutes trying to iron it out so it would look neat.

Marco wanted to take his dad's BMW because it was nicer than his mom's car. The BMW had a CD player, and Marco had spent more than an hour choosing the perfect CD. When he found out that his parents planned to go out that night and use the BMW, Marco was furious that he had to take the older car. The date hadn't even started, and already everything was going wrong.

Marco checked and rechecked his hair in the rearview mirror. Thinking that it looked too combed, he touched it again. Was it too messy?

When he got to Sabrina's house, he didn't know whether he should go in or not. He didn't want to meet her parents, and he thought that if he did they might ask him a lot of questions. But then again, if he didn't go inside, maybe her parents wouldn't trust him. Maybe they'd think he was rude. He ended up honking the horn three times, and Sabrina came out. He was so angry at himself for not going in that he hardly said two words to her in the car.

When they got to the party, he felt things were not going well at all. She seemed to be enjoying herself, but maybe she was just being kind. Maybe this was a charity date. Marco was so anxious at this point that he wished

8 | *he had something to calm him down. His friend Dave had brought a joint with him, and Marco decided to take a couple of hits, just to loosen up. He went to the bathroom and smoked half the joint. He felt a little better. He went over to the spiked punch bowl and started drinking. He was tired of thinking about the date, and he just wanted to enjoy himself. He felt that the alcohol was giving him the confidence he needed to talk to Sabrina. Finally, it seemed things were going all right.*

At about three in the morning, the party was winding down. Marco was so messed up he could hardly stand. The next thing he knew, Sabrina left with her friend Tracy, and she didn't even say goodbye. He ended up crashing on the couch. The next Monday in school, Marco was too embarrassed to talk to Sabrina. When she saw him, she looked the other way. What he had hoped would be a perfect date had turned out to be a night of humiliation.

This book explores the connection between perfectionism and drug abuse. While some teens may be satisfied when they try to do their best, the perfectionist is not. Like Marco, the perfectionist feels that even his best efforts don't measure

up. In his mind, he must always be in
control of everything he does. Otherwise
he thinks he is a total failure. It is this all-
or-nothing thinking that gets him into
trouble.

When teens like Marco believe that
they are not living up to the high expectations they or others have set for them,
they may turn to drugs. Drug abuse may
temporarily make a perfectionist feel okay
by masking his depression or anxiety, but
when the drug wears off, the problems
remain. And the teen may now have
another problem—chemical dependence,
or addiction.

In order to cope with these problems,
one must have a clear head. Recognizing
that perfectionism can be crippling is a
big step toward positive change. This
book discusses the problem of perfectionism: how it begins; why some teens turn
to drugs to solve the problem; and how
teens get trapped in a cycle of chemical
dependence. It also discusses where teens
can turn if they want to stop abusing drugs
and ways teens can cope more effectively
with the problem of perfectionism.

Even when a perfectionist does something well, he may feel that he is a failure.

CHAPTER 1

Defining Perfectionism

*D*oes it ever seem that your best efforts just aren't good enough? That no matter how well you do, you could have done better? We all feel that way from time to time. You tell yourself that you could have gotten straight A's, you could have kicked more field goals.

But perfectionists almost always tell themselves that they must do things perfectly. Since no one can do everything perfectly, perfectionists try to do the impossible. For that reason, they feel that they are constantly failing.

The perfectionist sees things in black and white. He feels that he must never make mistakes. If he comes in second, he

12 | is angry with himself for not coming in first. A perfectionist thinks that being less than perfect equals being a failure.

Even when perfectionists do succeed, their sense of achievement usually doesn't last long. Unable to feel good about themselves, they belittle their accomplishments. The star forward thinks, "Any fool could have scored that goal. The goalie was asleep." Or the girl in perfect shape who misses one day of workout thinks, "I just can't let my body go like this." Perfectionists tend to magnify their faults and minimize their good points.

Thinking Out of Control

When things don't go according to a perfectionist's plan, he feels he has lost control of the situation. He has "failed." Life is full of unpredictable moments, but the perfectionist can't accept that. Like Marco, he wants to control every detail of every moment.

Because a perfectionist pushes himself to be perfect, he is more likely to fail. The intense pressure he puts on himself may end up spoiling his performance. To spare himself the pain of trying and failing, he may end up failing on purpose without realizing it. That way, he can tell people,

A perfectionist may put so much pressure on himself that he undercuts his own performance.

"I told you so." And the perfectionist will be right. A top ball player who missed a free throw in the last game can tell himself he won't sink a single basket in the next game. And more often than not, he will unconsciously do as poorly as he told himself to.

An Attitude of Excellence

There is another kind of teen who strives for excellence. While the perfectionist must always be *the* best, a teen who strives for excellence works to do *his* best. He doesn't go to pieces when things don't go his way. If he doesn't perform a

13

14 task to perfection, he can take that in stride. He can look at his mistakes and learn from them so that next time he may do better. This is a much healthier attitude. When a teen takes his quest for excellence too far, he becomes a perfectionist.

All or Nothing

Many perfectionists have an "all-or-nothing" attitude. They believe that they must be either perfect or a failure. But since no one is perfect, perfectionists feel defeated more often than do people who have more realistic expectations. Perfectionists put so much pressure on themselves that they are afraid to try new things. They are afraid they will fail.

This all-or-nothing attitude can affect relationships too. Not accepting herself, the perfectionist finds it hard to believe that others do. She may keep people at a distance because she fears that they would reject her if they knew what she were really like. To hide her fear of being rejected and her feelings of shame, she may hold back from showing strong feelings. She may avoid developing emotional attachments. This may make her seem

A perfectionist may believe that if she is not as thin as a model, she is "ugly."

16 cold or distant. Feeling isolated and depressed, she may turn to drugs.

Sunita

It was Saturday night. Sunita, a high school junior, was at home watching MTV again. It was not that she didn't have opportunities to go out. In fact, a couple of decent guys were interested in her. But she wouldn't go out with them.

She was always telling herself, "I'm too fat! No one's going to like me." She was so ashamed of her looks that she didn't respect anyone who was attracted to her. Whenever anyone asked her out, she assumed that he was not worth dating. She agreed with Groucho Marx's comment that he would not want to be a member of any club that would accept him.

Sunita spent a lot of time feeling terrible about herself. She started drinking, mostly at home and by herself, but sometimes with her friend Julie. After a few drinks she could accept herself a little more. But then the alcohol would wear off and she would be left feeling awful.

In reality, Sunita was attractive and not overweight. But because she was not rail thin she felt bad about herself. For

Sunita, either she was thin like a model or ugly. Like most perfectionists, she had an all-or-nothing attitude.

Fear of Imperfection

When a perfectionist is in a situation where he doesn't know the rules, he often freezes up. Not knowing what is "right" and what is "wrong" makes him uncertain and causes him to feel anxious. If he makes the wrong move, he fears, his whole world may come tumbling down.

Because he fears to make the wrong move, the perfectionist often agonizes over decisions. He thinks that if only he had better information, he could make a good choice. Or he may think that he has too much information; everything seems to take on equal importance. He then has a hard time making a decision. The perfectionist may blame the information, either too much or too little, for his failure to make a decision or get his work done. But it is really his own fear of doing a less than perfect job.

Ben

Ben had one day to write a one-page report on the life of James Polk for history class. Most kids in the class thought it was a simple

18 *assignment. But Ben panicked. He went to the library immediately and checked out every book he could find on Polk. He read sections from each book. He scribbled notes frantically on a legal pad, and after forty-five minutes he had eight-and-a-half pages of notes. He started looking over his material, and every-thing seemed important. How could he boil it down to one page? When he got home he struggled to decide what would come first, what would come next, and what he would cut. Finally he sat down to write. In the morning he was bleary-eyed. Everything he had written the night before was in a crum-pled heap next to his computer. Nothing he wrote seemed right. He had not slept, he had no report, and he felt like a total failure. He swallowed two sleeping pills he found on his dad's dresser and slept until noon.*

Although you wouldn't know it from Ben's behavior, he is a straight A student. But his need to do a perfect job, to write the perfect paper, prevented him from writing any paper at all.

This, of course, is not always the case. Some perfectionists manage to be very productive, but they often complain that their work takes them much longer than it should. And they are probably right.

Believing that he must do a perfect job, a perfectionist may agonize over every assignment.

On the whole, perfectionists tend to focus more on details. They tend to be too thorough for their own good. Perfectionists often have very low self-esteem. Their way to try to feel better is to look perfect, to perform perfectly, to be perfect. When perfectionists see themselves missing the mark, they may become frustrated, anxious, and depressed.

Are You a Perfectionist?
As we've seen so far, perfectionism is a self-destructive way of thinking and

20 | behaving. Are you a perfectionist? Answer the following for yourself:

- Do you feel like a failure when you make even a small mistake?
- Do you think that if you can't do things really well you shouldn't do them at all?
- Do you feel anxious when you're in a new situation and you don't know what's expected of you?
- Do you need to know and follow rules to feel comfortable?
- Do you spend a lot of time trying to make decisions, only to second-guess them once you've made them?
- Do you worry that at any moment you may be "found out" as who you really are and may then be rejected?
- Do you often say to yourself, "I'm no good," and then feel like a failure?

If you answered yes to any of these questions, you may be letting perfectionism get the best of you.

CHAPTER 2

Childhood Causes of Perfectionism

*T*here are different ideas on the roots of perfectionism. Some believe that a teen inherits certain biological characteristics from his parents and that that makes him more likely to become a perfectionist. Scientists have yet to answer this question.

But one thing is certain. Early life experiences do play a major role in creating perfectionistic behavior. Chances are if you're a perfectionist now, you have been one for quite some time. As a child you looked to your parents to provide an example of how to act. A child tends to idealize his parents, seeing them as able to do no wrong because they can do for the child what he cannot do for himself.

Children are strongly shaped by their parents' expectations.

Gradually a child gains control over his world, learning to do such simple things as feeding himself.

At each new stage, the child needs encouragement from his parents. He needs to feel that he is loved unconditionally, that he can take risks and fail and still be loved. If a parent doesn't express affection or doesn't encourage the child, the child may think he is doing wrong. And if a parent regularly criticizes the child, making him feel that his best efforts are worthless, the child begins to feel like a failure.

The perfectionist thinks to himself, "If only I were a better person," or "If only I got better grades," or "If only my nose wasn't so big, then maybe my parents would love me." But a very demanding parent may rarely be pleased, especially if he or she was also criticized as a child. And so the child may begin a lifelong pattern of trying to meet impossible expectations. It's a no-win situation.

Mona

When she was growing up, Mona remembers, her mother was strict and unforgiving. Mona was often punished for being too loud, too messy, or just plain childlike.

24   *Mona recalls once playing with her building blocks. Her mother was in the next room preparing for guests. When her mother came out to check on Mona, she saw the blocks scattered on the floor and flew into a rage. She hated it when Mona messed up her livingroom. She made Mona pick up all the blocks and then sent her to her room "for not playing responsibly." Mona never saw those blocks again, and she didn't want to upset her mother by asking about them.*

When she started school, Mona was a cautious girl. Sometimes during recess she would stand off to the side while the other children played. Unless she knew the game, she would find any excuse not to play. She remembered all too well her mother's harsh words and punishment for not doing things just right.

By the time she was ten, Mona had figured out ways to please her mother, or at least not to make her angry. She could often go for days without being yelled at. In the meantime, Mona's mother began taking Valium, which is a sedative. Her doctor thought this would help her deal with her own stress.

Now Mona is in high school. She feels such a need for order that she often spends hours alone in her room. She puts her books

A teen who has grown up with unreasonable parental demands often puts the same kind of pressure on himself that his parents did.

26 | *in alphabetical order. She gets down on her hands and knees to pick up any stray lint or crumbs from the floor. In fact, she feels she can't go to sleep until this is done.*

Her #2 pencils are always sharpened, and her school locker is immaculate. She does everything "just right."

Yet Mona is unhappy. She takes her mother's Valium "just to feel normal." She thought that by keeping order, she could earn her mother's love and affection. But she is trapped in a cycle of trying to please her mother, feeling anxious that she'll fail, and using drugs to feel better.

In Mona's case, her mother's perfectionism and desperate need for her house to be in order led Mona to adopt the same thoughts and behaviors for herself. She was too young to see that her mother's behavior was unhealthy and irrational. Wanting to please her, Mona tried to fulfill her mother's quest for perfection at the expense of her own happiness.

Living Out a Parent's Dream

A parent may try to fulfill his own unrealized dreams through his child. For instance, he may have dreamed of becoming an actor himself, but instead he had

a family at a young age and had to get
a "real" job to support them. Now he
drives his teenage son around from audition to audition, hoping that his son lands
the role that will launch him to stardom.

When a child becomes a tool to fulfill
a parent's fantasies, pain and unhappiness
are the usual result. The child may feel
the parent's expectations keenly. He may
want desperately to please the parent.

Such pressure on a child often leaves
him little time just to be a kid. It is
harder for him to enjoy playing simply for
fun rather than for the sake of being
perfect. When a parent deprives a child of
such unpressured experiences, the child
may grow up to make the same unreasonable demands of himself that the parent
once made of him.

The Child's Place in the Family

Birth order is the order in which we are
born into a family. According to experts
on birth order, the perfectionist tends to
be a first-born or only child. Because her
parents had no child-rearing experience
before her, they may have been overly
cautious in raising her. They may have
tried not to make mistakes and worried
over her minor troubles. Overprotective

A perfectionist usually feels that if she is not in first place, she has failed.

parents may have made their child afraid to take risks.

Sometimes parents may give a child so much attention and be so delighted with every little thing she does that she may always feel onstage. That sort of attention and approval makes her feel good. But it may also create for her the need to seek approval from others instead of finding it within herself. Perfectionists often rely too much on what others think. Their sense of who they are is often lost in the need to please others.

Sibling rivalry, competition between brothers and sisters, may also contribute to the making of the perfectionist. For instance, Ivan and Nikolai are brothers, born three years apart. Their parents had been proud when Nikolai began to win swim meets. He came in first for three years in a row. Then his brother Ivan entered high school and showed a real knack for the sport. Swimming had earned Nikolai praise and attention. Now he thought he might have to share the limelight with his brother. He began to diet, exercise, and practice long hours. Swimming no longer held any enjoyment for him. But he couldn't stop. He feared he might lose his parents' love and respect.

30 | *Blaming Yourself*

Sometimes a child becomes a perfectionist because she is trying to compensate for the negative, unhealthy behavior of another family member. For instance, in a family where the father is constantly losing his temper and yelling at his family because he is feeling stressed, a child may believe that *she* is the cause of the problem. So she may go out of her way to take care of everyone and everything. The child does not realize that she is not the cause of the problem; changing her behavior will not solve the problem or change her father's behavior.

The stress of trying to hold the family together despite a parent's negative behavior can be very great. A teen may find herself turning to drugs for a temporary escape.

CHAPTER 3

Drugs and Perfectionism

*S*ensing that he is "no good" as he is, a perfectionist may feel that changing himself in some way will improve him. Maybe, he thinks, drugs can help him be perfect, or at least "normal."

Some teens believe that drugs can help them feel more confident, keep them focused on a task, or help them feel comfortable among other people. But by relying on drugs, a teen is actually making his original problems much worse. Drug abuse often brings addiction with it.

Some athletes use steroids in the mistaken belief that winning is more important than taking care of their bodies.

A perfectionist may not even realize that he has become dependent on a drug. He may think that he is in control and that his drug use just helps him to cope with his imperfections. But soon casual drug-taking may develop into addiction.

The perfectionist teen may turn to drugs for many reasons—to boost his performance, to relieve anxiety, to feel better about himself, or to relieve depression. Let's explore each of these reasons.

To Boost His Performance

Many perfectionists think they are what they achieve, so they may welcome anything that claims to improve their performance—even drugs. But they may become dependent on drugs.

Anabolic steroids are laboratory-made versions of the male sex hormone testosterone. They stimulate growth and accelerate weight gain. The perfectionist athlete may take these drugs to make him better able to compete. The athlete may come to rely on the drug to give him a sense of well-being and confidence. While he may think he has solved his problem—he finally feels okay about himself—below the surface, the perfectionist is just as unhappy as before. What's more, he is now caught up in a self-destructive habit.

In order to boost his energy, the perfectionist may turn to *amphetamines*, or uppers. Amphetamines are a class of drugs that speed up the body and brain. Perhaps the perfectionist has an important project to finish, and he feels tired—so he takes some speed to keep awake. This powerful stimulant will decrease his need to sleep and boost his ability to keep doing his project. Because of this surge of energy, he may feel that he can perform

A perfectionist who feels frustrated because he has not done a perfect job may turn to drugs because he does not know how to cope.

superhuman feats. The problem is that the need to feel "up" may cause him to take more and more drugs. He may continue to deprive himself of sleep, which his body needs. Soon he may become addicted.

To Relieve Anxiety

Many perfectionists turn to drugs to relieve anxiety. The intense pressure they put on themselves to live up to their own expectations may cause them severe stress and anxiety. When Ben tried to write the "perfect" report, he raised his expectations so high that no matter what he wrote, he was bound to fall short of his standard. He felt the frustration of not getting his report done, and this caused him to panic. That sort of anxiety can seem unbearable.

In order to reduce that anxiety, the perfectionist may turn to drugs. Marco, after worrying himself sick over his date, after beating himself up over every mistake he thought he had made, felt he had no choice but to seek release. He drank alcohol and smoked pot to reduce his anxiety.

Anxiety may prevent a perfectionist from approaching situations that make

Perfectionists who face anxiety-producing situations sometimes turn to drugs for relief.

him uncomfortable. He may go out of his way to avoid circumstances where he fears that he will not be successful. Or if he cannot avoid them, he may medicate himself with a drug so that he won't feel the pain. The perfectionist teen who fears making mistakes and being laughed at in public may get loaded before going to a party.

A perfectionist is often an expert procrastinator. He puts things off until it is too late. So he may feel anxious that he does not have time to complete an assignment. To control his anxiety he may take

a drink, toke on a joint, or swallow a
Valium when a deadline approaches.
Depending on the drug, the frequency of
use, and the amount, the teen who uses
drugs to control anxiety risks addiction.

To Relieve Anxiety About Appearance
Some perfectionists think it is not their
performance they must improve, but their
appearance. This type of perfectionist
believes that life would go her way if only
she looked "just so." The pressure of
needing to look perfect can make this sort
of perfectionist turn to drugs.

The cycle can go something like this:
The teen fears that she is not the "right"
weight. She takes diet pills to lose weight
and improve her self-image. But because
her perfectionism prevents her from ever
believing she has achieved the right
weight, she continues to take the drugs
despite the fact that they are hurting her.
She becomes addicted to them. And she
fears that she will gain weight if she stops
taking them.

Often the perfectionist who seeks total
control and turns to drugs loses the very
control she seeks to gain. Ironically, the
"solution" of using an addictive drug
backfires: Once someone becomes

38 addicted, she has lost control over the choice of whether or not to use a drug.

To Relieve Depression

For a perfectionist, anxiety can often lead to depression. When approaching a task, the perfectionist may want so badly to do it perfectly that he becomes frantic at the prospect of failing. But after he has either "failed" at the task or avoided it completely and the anxiety about the task has subsided, he may feel depressed.

He may turn to drugs such as cocaine or amphetamines to elevate his depressed mood. Or he may seek to numb the pain with alcohol, sleeping pills, or tranquilizers. The drugs may be different, but the underlying need is the same—to feel acceptable.

Drugs Don't Solve It

Instead of addressing the problem of perfectionism, drug abuse ignores it, sweeping the problem under the carpet. But drug abuse is far more dangerous than the problems of perfectionism. Just what those dangers are is the focus of the next chapter.

CHAPTER 4

The Reality of Drugs

*A*s we saw, Marco's desire to have the perfect date with Sabrina caused him to sabotage his evening. He was so anxious that he felt he had to get wasted just to cope.

Three months after Marco's date with Sabrina, he saw her with another guy. The couple were walking down the school hallway arm in arm. Marco felt sick inside. When he got home that afternoon, he stole a fifth of whiskey from his dad's liquor cabinet, went to his room, and drank until he couldn't see straight.

The next day he woke up at noon with a splitting headache. He fell asleep again and slept until three. He had an exam to prepare   **39**

Although abusing drugs may offer a perfectionist temporary relief from feeling bad about herself, drug abuse creates many new problems.

for the next day, but he didn't much care. He told his parents that he had stomach flu. That would excuse him for a couple of days. In reality, he was angry at himself for having lost control at the party in front of Sabrina. He figured that's why she was with this other guy.

Maybe at that party he just drank a little too much booze, he thought. Maybe he just needed to find the "right" amount. Maybe if he had just a little buzz all the time, he would be more relaxed and carefree.

For the rest of the semester, Marco kept drinking, and occasionally he'd do coke.

Once a B student, Marco saw his grades plummet. Now, his perfectionism was no longer his main problem; drugs were.

Psychological and Physical Dependence

Abuse of any drug to deal with anxiety or depression can create *psychological dependence* on the drug. That means that a user believes he needs the drug just to get through a situation. He craves its effects.

Physical dependence also occurs in many drug users. The user's brain and body become so used to the drug that the user must keep using the drug in order to function.

Psychological and physical dependence on a drug is known as chemical dependence, or addiction. It can destroy a user's life.

Following is a description of some of the drugs that perfectionist teens turn to.

Alcohol

Many perfectionists drink before or during social events to cope with their anxiety. Others may drink in response to depression. *Tolerance* to alcohol and other drugs develops with continued use. A

42 | user needs more and more of the drug to achieve the same effects.

Alcohol abuse slows down the body. That is the reason it is so frequently the cause of fatal car accidents. It can also result in alcoholism.

Marijuana

At low doses, marijuana acts as a stimulant, something that speeds up the body. The user may experience heightened sense perception and a feeling of well-being. These effects may then give way to sedation, a slowing down of bodily functions. At higher doses, users often experience slowed reflexes, impaired judgment, and disturbed thought patterns. Heavy users often have problems learning, thinking, remembering, and problem-solving.

Anabolic Steroids

Steroids increase endurance and muscle tone. But they also damage the body. In men, withered testicles, impotence, enlargement of the breasts, premature baldness, and severe acne are only some of the symptoms associated with frequent steroid abuse. Women may suffer irregular menstruation, breast shrinkage, deepening of the voice, and growth of body and facial hair.

Users may easily become frustrated and perform poorly. Steroids may also induce anger and aggression. This is commonly known as "roid rage." In a few cases steroids have even brought on psychotic reactions, a loss of contact with reality.

Sedatives: Tranquilizers and Sleeping Pills

These drugs are legally prescribed by physicians to relieve anxiety and promote sleep, but they are often obtained illegally on the street. There they're known as "downers," "goofballs," "barbs," "blue devils," and "yellow jackets."

Sedatives can induce slurred speech, staggering, tremors, slowed heart and breathing rates, impaired memory, irritability, and depression. Very large doses can result in coma or can stop brain functions. Taking the drug with alcohol heightens the effect of sedation, increasing the risks of overdose and death.

In addition, someone who has developed a tolerance for these drugs should stop using them *only under medical supervision*. Otherwise the risk of a coma or death is very high.

Many legal drugs and nutritional supplements that are beneficial when used correctly are harmful when they are abused.

Cocaine and Crack

Cocaine and crack are highly addictive and are stimulants. Stimulants speed up the body. They increase the heart rate and blood pressure and suppress the appetite.

Crack is one of the most addictive of all drugs. Crack and cocaine have been known to cause heart failure, brain seizures, violent and paranoid behavior, and strokes.

Amphetamines

Amphetamines are stimulants. On the street they're known as "speed," "crank," "ice," "cross-tops," "whites," "black beauties," and "uppers." Amphetamines are found in certain diet pills.

Heavy users may suffer from vitamin deficiencies and malnutrition because they do not eat properly. Amphetamines have been known to cause dry mouth, blurred vision, irregular heartbeat, tremors, loss of coordination, brain damage, paranoia, and collapse. Amphetamine abuse has been directly linked to death by heart failure, high fever, or stroke.

Heroin

The risks of heroin use are extreme. The temporary feeling of euphoria that follows

46 injection of heroin often gives way to rest-lessness, nausea, and vomiting.

Since users can never be sure how weak or powerful the heroin is that they've bought on the street, the risk of overdosing is great. Convulsions, coma, and death may result.

Heroin users who share needles are at high risk of contracting HIV, liver disease, and hepatitis.

Heroin is highly addictive. Breaking the routine of heroin abuse for as little as one day can induce severe symptoms of withdrawal in an addict—chills, sweating, aches and pains, and muscle spasms. Tolerance to the drug develops, so the user must use more and more for the desired effects. This increases the risk of overdose.

Hallucinogens

Hallucinogens include many drugs, such as LSD, mescaline, and peyote. These drugs cause users to see, hear, and feel things that are not real. For that reason, when a person is high on a hallucinogen, it is impossible for him to think clearly or behave normally.

Hallucinogens are often contaminated with other drugs, and users never know whether they will have a "bad trip." This is a terrifying experience in which the user has frightening hallucinations. A bad trip can produce paranoia, depression, and panic.

Drug abuse does not bring a perfectionist closer to a solution for his problems. It only confuses his thinking and destroys his body. There are, however, ways out of the perfectionism–drug abuse cycle.

A drug-abusing teen who is a perfectionist usually has trouble admitting that she needs help.

CHAPTER 5

Seeking Help

For many people, perfectionism and drug abuse go hand in hand. It is important to treat both problems. If a person seeks help ending his drug abuse but continues to be a perfectionist, it is more likely that he will start using drugs again in the future to deal with his perfectionism. If he treats only his perfectionism, he will still have a destructive drug habit.

The drug-dependent perfectionist must first admit to himself that he has a problem. It is not uncommon for a teen to deny and conceal his drug use. He may try to persuade himself and others that he knows what's best for him and that things are under control. It is especially difficult

50 for many perfectionists to seek help. However, admitting that he needs help is the starting point for positive change.

Most experts agree that the drug problem must be treated before the perfectionism. If a teen is to make fundamental changes in his thoughts and behavior, he needs a clear head to do it. Drugs just confuse the issue.

Kicking the Drug Habit

A wide variety of treatment is available for drug abusers who seek it. Groups like Alcoholics Anonymous, Narcotics Anonymous, and Cocaine Anonymous may give teens the structured approach and group support they need to combat the drug problem. The advantage of support groups is that teens may find strength in numbers. This can help them deal with perfectionism too. And when others share their experiences, shy teens may find it easier to open up.

Alternately, you may turn to individual or family counseling. Individual counseling allows you to address your needs one-on-one with a therapist. And when perfectionism is compounded with drug abuse, individual attention may meet your needs better. Family therapy may be

useful for those whose perfectionism is
made worse by their home life. In such
situations, all family members are
involved, either individually or as a group.

51

You can also turn to school guidance
counselors and community service centers. If guidance counselors cannot help,
they can recommend a group or center
that does provide such help. Community
centers often sponsor programs on substance abuse prevention and treatment.
Many of the referral networks listed at the
end of this book can recommend such
centers.

Some people find that a clergy
member's spiritual guidance motivates
them to make positive changes in their
lives. If the clergy member has worked
with substance abusers before, he or she
will be better equipped to handle the situation. What's more, religious faith may
give the teen a way to understand and
cope with his perfectionism.

But whatever the source of help, you
need to recognize that recovering from
your drug habit and perfectionistic
thoughts will not take place overnight.
You must make a commitment to change.
You must be patient with yourself.

Allowing yourself to concentrate on the process of doing something—rather than on the results—will help you to reduce unreasonable expectations of perfection.

Undoing Perfectionism

What brings many teens to drugs in the first place is perfectionism. Once a teen quits drugs, he may not see an improvement in his thoughts and behavior. In fact, he may think that things are worse than before he started taking drugs. That is why the perfectionist also needs to work on changing his destructive thoughts and behavior.

Seeing perfectionism for what it is—a constant desire to reach unrealistic goals —may make it okay for you to relax your impossible standards. By aiming just to do your best, you can often ease the self-imposed pressure that has caused you so much fear of failure. You will probably do better than you think, simply because you allow yourself to. And once you concentrate less on results and more on the process, you may actually find you enjoy what you're doing.

Here are some practical ways to work on boosting your self-esteem. Remember, they may not be easy, because you are used to being hard on yourself. But with a commitment to change, you *will* see results. Just be patient with yourself. Cultivating a positive self-image is a day-to-day process.

54 | *Power of the Positive*

Self-talk, the constant conversation we have in our head, is very powerful. When we say to ourselves, "I stink, I'm no good," this has a very strong effect on us. Such thoughts will doom us to fail. But just as negative thoughts affect us greatly, so can positive thoughts. If you tell yourself, "I have something to offer. I am a valuable person. I can become the person I want to be," you will feel better about yourself. You will allow yourself the freedom to change. As corny as it sounds, thoughts of success *do* help people to succeed.

The process of replacing habitual negative thoughts with positive thoughts is sometimes known as thought reversal. Instead of concentrating on your weaknesses, concentrate on your strengths.

Set Realistic Goals

The next time you want to achieve something, like performing well on an exam, set a realistic goal. Don't aim for perfection; strive for excellence. Instead of thinking, "If I don't get 100% on that exam, I'm a failure," think, "I am going to do the best I can on this exam. If I make mistakes, that's okay."

Rather than focusing on past failures, see failures for what they are: learning experiences. They teach us what not to do in the future. There's an old saying, "Each failure brings us one step closer to success." Once you accept failure as part of the process of becoming the person you want to be, you will feel freer to take risks. And more than likely, you will succeed where you once feared you might fail.

Live in the Moment

Someone who constantly thinks of past mistakes or possible future mistakes never gets anywhere. He or she freezes up, feeling depressed and anxious. But you can choose a different path.

Remember, you cannot change the past. And if you focus on fear of failing in the future, you will miss the opportunities of the here and now. Live in the present. Have confidence in yourself and in your ability to make good decisions today. When your mind is focused on the present, you are better able to walk through a day with confidence, solving problems with a clear head. And each time you solve a problem, you will feel better about yourself.

Break Down a Task

56

When you see a great big task before you, do you think, "How will I ever finish this? I don't even know where to begin." You may feel overwhelmed. But there is a trick to tackling a task: Break it down into smaller tasks. Then do each one.

Remember Ben, who couldn't write his paper? He kept focusing on the result. The next time he has to write a report he could focus on the process instead. He could even write down the steps he needs to do to write the paper:

- Choose a topic
- Write a topic sentence
- Figure out what the main points of my paper will be
- See how much information I have about each of the main points
- Write the introduction, telling what the paper will discuss
- Write about each of the main points
- Write the conclusion, telling what the paper discussed

By thinking about each step, it is easier to do the task. By focusing on the process and not on getting an A, he stands a better chance of getting that A.

Ending Drug Abuse and Perfectionism | *57*

You can stop abusing drugs and can overcome your habit of perfectionism. It is not easy for a perfectionist to admit the need for help in kicking the drug habit. But for your own sake, it is important to admit this to yourself and recognize that it is okay to need help.

By developing a positive self-image, you will not only be able to deal more effectively in life without drugs. You will also be able to set realistic goals and accomplish them. Most important, you will feel better about yourself, flaws and all.

Glossary—
Explaining New Words

amphetamines   Powerful stimulants.

anabolic steroids   Laboratory-made versions of the male sex hormone testosterone.

barbiturates   Powerful drugs that slow down the central nervous system, medically prescribed to treat anxiety and sleeplessness.

euphoria   A feeling of elation.

physical dependence   A state in which the body adapts to a drug and needs it in order to function; not taking the drug brings on withdrawal—often tremors, sweating, vomiting, and chills—which lasts until the body gets used to doing without the drug.

psychological dependence   A mental craving for the pleasurable effects of a drug; a sense that one "needs" a drug to cope.

sedatives   Drugs that are legally prescribed to relieve anxiety and promote sleep; tranquilizers and sleeping pills.

stimulant   A substance that speeds up certain functions of the body and brain.

tolerance   The need to take more and more of a drug to achieve the effects originally achieved by smaller doses.

Where to Go for Help

Alcohol Treatment Referral Hot Line
1-800-ALCOHOL
Provides help and referrals for people
with concerns about alcohol or drug
use. (24 hours a day)

**Alcoholics Anonymous World
Services, Inc.**
212-870-3400
Provides information about AA and
worldwide referrals to local meetings.

American Self-Help Clearinghouse
http://www.cmhc.com/selfhelp
Provides links to over a thousand self-
help and support groups online.

Cocaine Hotline
1-800-COCAINE
Provides treatment referrals and some
drug information. (24 hours a day)

Marijuana Anonymous World Services
1-800-766-6779
Provides information about MA and
referrals to local meetings. (24 hours a
day, voice mail)

Narcotics Anonymous
818-773-9999
http://www.netwizards.net/recovery/na/

National Institute on Drug Abuse
1-800-662-HELP
Can link the caller to a variety of hot
lines that provide treatment referrals.

Recovery Online
http://www.netwizards.net/recovery/
index.html
Self-help groups and other recovery links
online.

For Further Reading

Ignoffo, Matthew, Ph.D. *Everything You Need to Know about Self-Confidence*. New York: Rosen Publishing Group, 1996.

Wilkinson, Beth. *Drugs and Depression*. New York: Rosen Publishing Group, 1994.

Challenging Reading

Adderholdt-Elliott, M.R. *Perfectionism: What's Bad about Being Too Good*. Minneapolis: Free Spirit Publishing Co., 1987.

Howarth, Enid, and Tras, Jan. *The Joy of Imperfection*. MN: Fairview Press, 1996.

Mallinger, Allan E., M.D., and De Wyze, Jeannette. *Too Perfect*. New York: Clarkson N. Potter, Inc., 1992.

Index

63

About the Author

Michael B. Langer is a freelance writer and teaches English as a second language in New York.

Photo Credits

Cover by John Novajosky; p. 2 by Olga M. Vega; p. 10 by Young-Hee Chia; pp. 13, 34, 48 by Lauren Piperno; pp. 15, 22, 36, 44 by Ira Fox; p. 19 by Kim Sonsky; pp. 25, 40 by Kathleen McClancy; pp. 28, 32, 52 by Skjold Photography.